Felizli Kidz

Bible ABCs at a Glance

ELIZABETH SABLON

WESTBOW
PRESS®
A DIVISION OF THOMAS NELSON
& ZONDERVAN

WestBow Press books may be ordered through booksellers or by contacting:

WestBow Press
A Division of Thomas Nelson & Zondervan
1663 Liberty Drive
Bloomington, IN 47403
www.westbowpress.com
1 (866) 928-1240

ISBN: 978-1-5127-7701-7 (sc)
ISBN: 978-1-5127-7700-0 (e)

Library of Congress Control Number: 2017902977

Print information available on the last page.

WestBow Press rev. date: 04/13/2017

Angel

Luke 1:26–29

My dear child, let me tell you a story of when God sent the angel Gabriel to Nazareth, a town in Galilee. There lived a young, beautiful girl pledged to be married to a man named Joseph. This man was a descendant of King David. The young girl's name was Mary, and God loved her very much. The angel, a messenger of God, said, "Greetings. God has found you to be beautiful inside and out. The Lord is with you." For this reason, the Lord has chosen you to be a vessel to bring to this world the redeemer of humanity. You will call his name Jesus.

Explain the story of the annunciation of God's promise, the birth of a child, Jesus, who was going to save and change the world. Tell your child about his special mission—to save us.

Angel

Baptism

Mathew 3:11

After Jesus grew up, he went to the Jordan River, where John the Baptist, his cousin, was baptizing people with water. Jesus went into the river and walked up to John so that he could baptize him. When John saw Jesus, he recognized him as the Son of the living God. The Holy Spirit descended on Jesus as John baptized him.

Explain to your child the sacrament of baptism and when he or she was baptized and why. Tell your child that this is his or her inheritance from you.

Baptism

Cross

John 3:16

When God created us, he had a perfect plan for all humans. God wanted us to live in a very wonderful place called the garden of Eden. Because the devil tricked us into disobeying God, we no longer live in that garden. However, God's love is so great that he allowed his Son, Jesus, to come to Earth and rescue us from our disobedience. Jesus died so that we could have life and a place next to our Father, God. The cross taken by Jesus is what restores us and through which a way is open to go back to that perfect place.

Explain how Jesus's mission is to make us whole again and how he completed it when he gave his life for us.

Cross

Liliana!

Denarius

Mark 12:14–17

One day, Jesus was meeting with his friends, the disciples, and others. Someone said to him, "Teacher, we know you are a good man. You are just to all and treat all men and women equally, and you are teaching us according to God's truth. Let me ask you this: Is it right to pay taxes to Caesar or not? Should we pay or shouldn't we?" During Jesus's time, people used a type of coin called a denarius to pay for taxes, food, clothing, and other things.

Jesus knows everyone's thoughts and intentions. He knew that the questioner wanted to trick him. Jesus told the man to bring him a denarius so that he could take a look at it. Once Jesus looked at the coin, he asked whose picture was on the coin and who wrote the inscription on the coin. "It is Caesar's," the crowd answered. Then Jesus told them, "Give to Caesar what it Caesar's and God what is God's."

Take a coin and explain how we also have to pay taxes and use coins—money to pay for goods and services. Also explain that money only pays for earthly things because material things are made by people. However, God demands people's hearts. That which is of the spirit belongs to God. Explain that God wants our hearts to follow him, and following him makes Jesus the center of our lives.

Denarius

Eating

Romans 14:17–18

The heavens rejoice whenever someone who disobeys decides to obey and follow Jesus. A party is thrown, and all the angels sing. But, "The Kingdom of God is not a matter of eating and drinking, but of righteousness, peace and joy in the Holy Spirit, because anyone who serves Christ in this way is pleasing to God and approved by men."

Explain that as we follow Jesus in obedience, we are also eating of the promise of never-ending life in the kingdom of God and that God promises to be with us always.

Eating

Fruit

Galatians 5:22–23

As we decide to be followers of Jesus, a light shines out of our innermost being. This light gives way to qualities that flourish into love, joy, peace, patience, kindness, goodness, faithfulness, gentleness, and self-control. All these fruits flow from us and turn us into beacons of light that others want to be a part of.

Explain that we are not talking about fruits that we eat but rather those that are given by the Holy Spirit. We receive the fruits of the Spirit as we continue in obedience to the Lord, and in turn we become wiser.

Fruit

Gardener

John 15:1–4 and Galatians 5:22–23

God is the gardener of his creation—us. God planted the tree of life in his Son, Jesus, and we are the branches. As long as we stay connected to him, we will bear the fruit of joy, peace, patience, kindness, goodness, faithfulness, gentleness, and self-control because we are rooted in him.

Take your child outside and show him or her the branches on a tree. Explain that in the same way that a branch is connected to a tree, we are also connected to Jesus. That connection exists because he paid for our sins on the cross. The Word of God is what keeps us attached to him.

Gardener

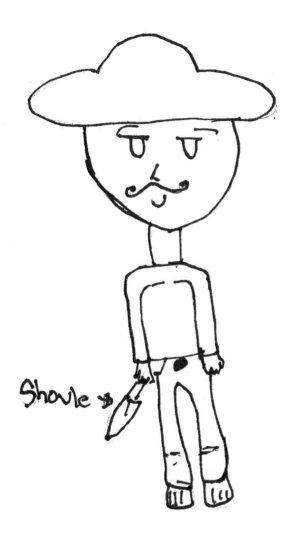

Shovle ✗

Helmet

Isaiah 59:17

God sent many special people called prophets to talk to us and teach us that when we listen to God's instruction and keep his teachings in our hearts, those teachings become a helmet of protection. When we listen to the Lord, we become wiser and make better decisions; we obey. "He put on righteousness as his breastplate, and the helmet of salvation on his head."

Explain that the Word of the Lord is our armor and helmet to go through life. He has given us the Word to protect us in this world.

Helmet

Infant

Matthew 21:16

Jesus came to the world as an infant. God chose to have Jesus come as a little person to do big things for us, his children. Infants hold a very special place in God's heart because "from the lips of children and infants you have ordained praise."

Say, "You, my child, are a blessing, and the Lord listens because you believe in him."

Infant

Jesus

Revelation 22:20

God promised that one day he would send someone very special to lead the way back to our Father in heaven. He sent Jesus to give us directions and show the path we should take to bring us back to heaven. Jesus is the promise that was talked about for many generations, and he will return.

Jesus is the promised Messiah who came and who will return. Tell your child that Jesus is coming back to take us to heaven to be with our Father.

Jesus

Keys

Matthew 16:19

A key is a small tool that is used to open a door that is closed or to turn on a car—a key can be used to unlock things. One day while Jesus was talking to his friends, he promised Peter that because he believed him to be the Son of God, Peter would receive a key that would interpret—unlock—God's Word to his lost children.

The Holy Spirit revealed to Peter the truth about Jesus, who left the key to heaven. All we need to do is follow him.

Keys

Liliana!

Lamb

John 1:29

Remember when John the Baptist looked up while in the Jordan River and saw Jesus? He recognized him and said, "Look, the Lamb of God, who takes away the sin of the world!" He will show us the way back to our Father in heaven.

Explain that Jesus was the promise that many prophets had written about in the Old Testament as our Redeemer and Messiah. He offers himself so that we can live.

Lamb

Mustard Seed

Matthew 17:20

There was a group of people surrounding Jesus when a man came and asked Jesus to heal his son, who was sick. Jesus helped the man's son and healed him. Jesus later told his friends that when you have faith as small as seed of mustard "nothing will be impossible for you."

Explain that Jesus promised that with faith all will be given according to the Father's will. That's why Jesus tells us that when we have faith as small as a mustard seed, we can move mountains. This could be the mountain of fear.

Mustard Seed

Name

Matthew 18:20

Names have great meanings. Your name is what it is because we decided to name you with that name. God, for example, named his Son Jesus. He named him Jesus because he came to show us the way back to our Father in heaven. One day during a meeting with his friends, Jesus told them that whenever two or more met in his name he too would be present, "for where two or three come together in my name, there am I with them." That is a powerful promise!

Tell your child right now, as we read together, Jesus is with us because he promised that when two or more are together in his name he too will be there.

Name

Omega

Revelation 1:8

God was never created and will always be. "I am the Alpha and the Omega," says the Lord God, "who is, and who was, and who is to come, the Almighty."

The Lord knows all and will always be.

Omega

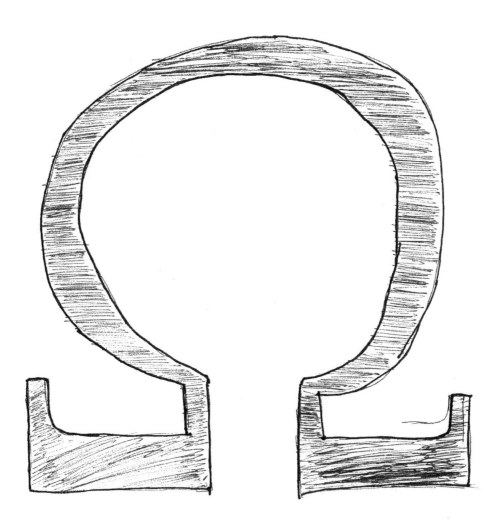

Pillar

1 Timothy 3:15

A pillar is a structure used in buildings. The pillar serves as a support for the building so it will stand firm and will not fall. God gave us his Word as a pillar so that we will know what is right and what is wrong and all people will live in peace. "If I am delayed, you will know how people ought to conduct themselves in God's household, which is the church of the living God, the pillar and foundation of the truth."

Explain how God has giving us the building blocks for our lives. He is the pillar and foundation of the church----us—because he alone is the only truth. His Word is the blueprint and instructions to be a guide for life.

Pillar

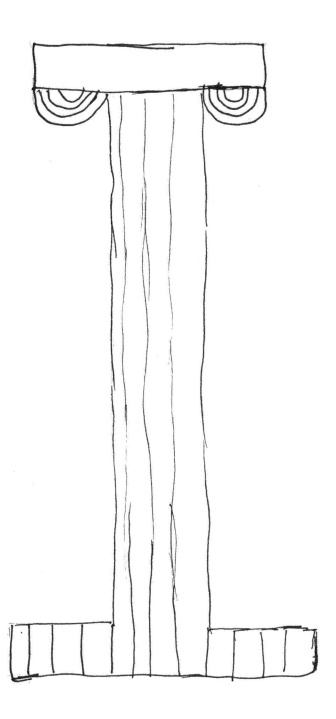

Quiet

Psalm 23:2

Quiet time is important in everybody's life because it allows us to have a moment to talk to the Lord. The Holy Spirit will interpret what we are saying during this time. "He makes me lie down in green pastures; He leads me beside quiet waters. He restores my soul."

Use this moment to stay quiet and to talk to God and his beloved Son, Jesus.

Quiet

Root

Isaiah 53:2

Roots are the way living plants receive food. The food is used for energy so the plant can grow healthy, whole, and beautiful. God's Word nourishes his children in the same way that food keeps us healthy, whole, and beautiful—inside and out. "He grew up before him like a tender shoot, and like a root out of dry ground. He had no beauty or majesty to attract us to him, nothing is in his appearance that should desire him."

Discuss the importance of trusting in your inner beauty.

Root

Seed

Luke 8:5–8

Seeds are used to grow plants for food and to make our homes beautiful with flowers. Before a farmer can plant seed, he or she has to use good soil, plow the soil, and water it so the seed will grow into a beautiful healthy plant. God's Word is the good soil, the water, and the light that make our hearts grow beautiful. As we listen and follow him, we will grow in strength and inner beauty. "Still other seed fell on good ground soil. It came up and yielded a crop, a hundred times more than sown."

Do a little experiment. Take two seeds of beans and plant them in separate pots. Let one be nourished with water and light but not the other one. Observe the outcome on each. Explain that the seed is talking about us and that the Word of God is what nourishes each of us in the same way that the light and water helps the plant grow.

Seed

Temple

1 Corinthians 3:16

A temple is a building used to worship. When God created our bodies, He designed them to be his temple. God lives in our hearts and maintains and sustains us. The Holy Spirit is always speaking to us because God lives in us. "Don't you know that you yourselves are God's temple and that God's Spirit lives in you?"

Explain how God lives in your child's body. We need to take care of it by paying attention to what we see, listen to, and speak.

Temple

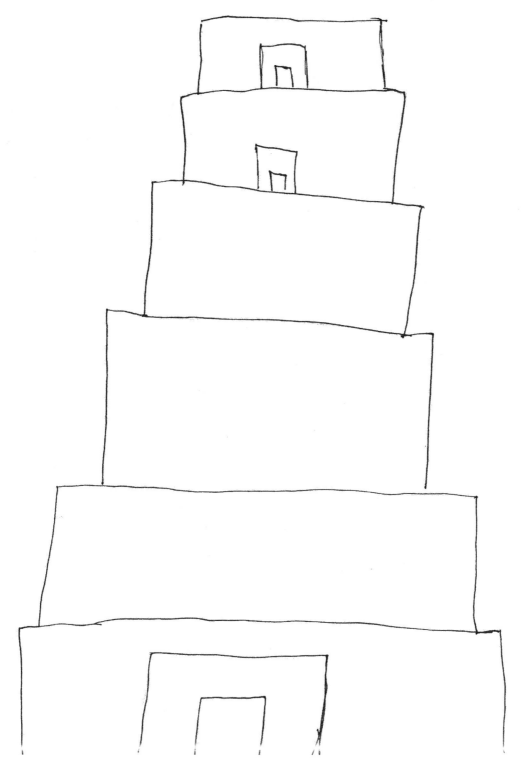

Universe

Philippians 2:14–16

The universe was created by God. The universe has many galaxies, planets and stars. You are one of those stars! Each of us was created to be a beacon of light to shine and lead others to the light. God tells us, "Do everything without complaining or arguing, so that you may become blameless and pure, children of God without fault."

You are a star. You have your own light that shines very bright to the world, the light that the Lord gave you when he formed you.

Universe

Valley

Psalm 23:4

A valley is a place that is surrounded by mountains, and a river that runs through it. It is usually flat and without many obstacles, but before you can get to it you have to go through tall, dangerous mountains. But you can trust that God will be with you every step of the way. Getting to the valley may not be easy, but he will be with you always. "Even though I walk through the shadow of the valley of death, I fear no evil, for you are with me; your rod and your staff, they comfort me."

Explain how God has promised that even when we are going through a hard time at home or with friends he is with us! He is our comfort and strength.

Valley

Wings

Isaiah 40:30–31

Wings are what birds and airplanes use to fly. Wings of freedom are what God gave you when his Son, Jesus, died for us. Everybody gets tired and make mistakes, "but those who hope in the Lord will renew their strength. They will soar on wings like eagles; they will run and not grow weary, they will walk and not be faint."

Acknowledge that all of us make mistakes, but we have the Lord who is our strength. Remember the promise that by grace you are forgiven!

Wings

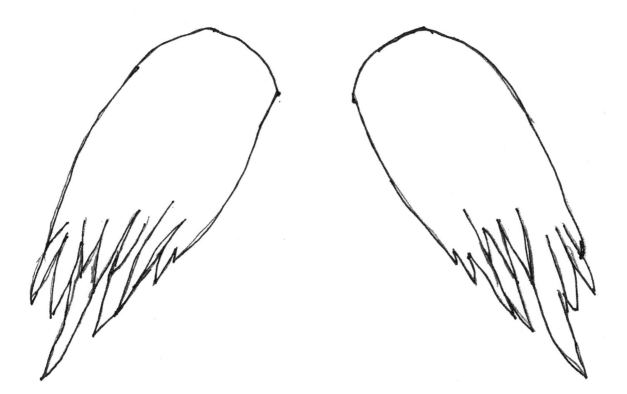

X—Gates to Heaven

John 14:6

Imagine looking at the firmament and seeing a giant letter *x*. Then, imagine something magical happening—the letter is not a letter but rather a giant gate, and as you stare, it starts to open! It grows larger and larger, and then you realize that those are the gates of heaven where you see the Lord inviting you in. "I am the way and the truth and the life. No one comes to the Father except through me."

Tell your child that Jesus is showing us the way to join him in heaven. The cross is the gate to heaven. God's Word is the path, and Jesus is the key!

X—Gates to Heaven

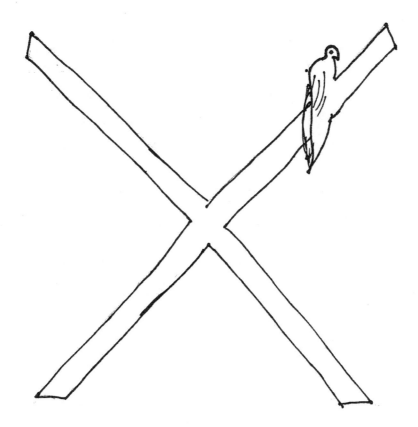

Yoke

Mathew 11:29

A yoke is a wooden tool that is fastened around the necks of two oxen that share the weight of the yoke. This tool is attached to a plow that the oxen pull and that allows them to work together to work the soil in the fields in preparation for planting seeds. We, too, are all called and have a mission to go out into the world and work together to spread the good news, that we are loved by God! In other words, we must plant the seed of love so others know that he too loves them. "Take my yoke upon you and learn from me, for I am gentle and humble in heart, and you will find rest for your souls. For my yoke is easy and my burden is light."

Jesus walks with us in moments of trouble. He changes our hearts! Having him by our side makes all troubles lighter because he is helping us carry the weight.

Yoke

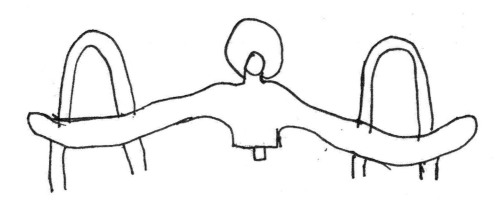

Zion

Romans 9:33

Jesus is the rock and foundation of a fruitful life. He is our place of refuge, and he will always protect us. It is written, "See, I lay in Zion a stone that causes men to stumble and a rock that makes them fall, and the one who trusts in him will never be put to shame."

God's promises are true forever. That is why Jesus is the rock of Zion. He is the true foundation for life.

Zion